ISSN 1749-4

EAST KENT

POETRY REVIEW

NO. 2   SPRING 2006

The East Kent Poetry Review is published twice a year in Ramsgate and distributed throughout Kent. It is non-profit making, and associated with the East Kent Poetry Society, which is also based in Ramsgate, and which meets every two weeks to read out poems and engage in friendly discussion.

SPLIT THE LARK
POETRY FESTIVAL
DEAL AND DOVER
POETRY COMPETITION
FIRST PRIZE £250,
SECOND PRIZE £150,
THIRD £75
ADJUDICATOR:
JOHN WHITWORTH

No entry form required. Poems up to a maximum of 40 lines, each to be typed on a single side of A4 paper. A separate sheet should contain the titles of poems, name address and phon number of entran Entry fee £3 one poem, £5 for tw £10 for fiv Cheques payable 'Split The Lark Poe Liz Tur 1 King Edward Deal, Kent CT14 Tel 01304 38

CLOSING D 30TH APRIL

LYNNE REES

CONTENTS

EDITORIAL

Society & Journal

Owing to the overwhelming number of contributions to this, the second edition of the EKPR, the main editorial problem has been to fit everyone in.

However, I was very pleased that Lynne Rees, distinguished 'local' poet (by adoption), agreed to provide four poems for the 'spotlight' feature.

Thanks to Marion Nelson, the EKPR is being distributed extensively throughout East Kent and even beyond, reaching out to the badlands of Maidstone, Tunbridge Wells and Medway. Who knows, one day a copy might even reach the Far West of Bromley and Sevenoaks.

Many people have written to express their appreciation of the Review, and it has been heartening to receive support from librarians and booksellers around the county.

This edition has less prose commentary in it, because of the abundance of poetry. I am not sure whether to regret the diminution of critique, or rejoice. I suppose the poems can speak for themselves, and at this rate the Review may have to become a quarterly.

LETTERS TO THE EDITOR

Sir,
In your article *Poetry On The Radio* you talked about digital radio channels which have occasional poetry readings, which you called 'fillers.' How can I find out more about that?

F. Thompson, Whitstable.

- The Guardian has a good radio listings and review section, but the Radio Times has the best listings for Oneword. Then there's the internet – the BBC website provides info about poetry programmes, and if you have something called RealPlayer (a free download), you can access archives. The Oneword site has a chat room. But unfortunately, the only way to catch 'fillers' is to listen to Oneword and wait for gaps in the programming.

Sir,
Thank you for producing a local poetry review. I enjoyed the mix of poetry and comment. I'm wondering how you select the poems and articles?

Mrs A Wynstanton, Deal.

- The aim of the *Review* is to reflect the work of people in East Kent, and to be as inclusive as possible. As more people offer poems and comments, that inclusiveness will become more difficult, and the arbitrary interventions of editorship may come into play.

SPECIAL FEATURE

FOUR POEMS BY LYNNE REES.

what's happening

my clock is throwing its voice across the room
my laptop starts its heavy breathing
the desk-lamp is busy
bleaching a patch on the wall

while I do nothing – just lie here and watch
a candle flame stretch
and bounce off molecules of air
an insect lit by the evening sun jumping at the
                                    windowpane

this morning when I opened the sash
a single spider thread slung from the sill
propping up the weight of the wooden frame –
no wonder

I had to lie back down
listen to the sighs of my un-sipped inch of tea
bubbles in the water carafe gossiping at the
                                    glass
an apple on my dresser one long golden yawn

SPECIAL FEATURE

FOUR POEMS BY LYNNE REES

The Crazies

We used to think they were foxes haunting the
Now we know better –   [night.

how they rise in the middle of storms, excited
by the thunder and crack, close in

easy as flood water over open land,
their wails raising the hairs on our arms.

And we know how to protect ourselves,
how we should close the windows, bolt the ddors,

how we should breathe slowly,
block our ears against their pleading,

our mouths from shouting back and urging them on.
But one of us always lets them in.

The morning after
we talk lightly about milk, road-works,

look past each other, eyes
raw with the night's unrest. It'll be days

before we dare to check the horizon, forget
who opened the door.

SPECIAL FEATURE

Fat

Skinny women order his fish
fried in low-cholesterol oil,
batter as crisp and sheer as glass.

He teases them about goose-fat,
the slip of it, how it dimples
under fingertips, at the right point
of tenderness how it gives
to the tip of a tongue.

He dreams of women
whose flesh parts for him
like lard – their overlap, the spill
and pleat of them, his hands skating
over their suety gleam, their excess
rejoicing under his palms.

SPECIAL FEATURE

FOUR POEMS BY LYNNE REES

Like Water

A tendon flickers in your wrist like an eel
then flits between the channel of bones,
the pulse at the side of your bones
checks your heart's tide of blood, breath
ripples in your sleeping throat, and this reminds me
how sometimes you are like a great wave
rushing me along the coast of your life,
and other times like the shadowed corner of a pool,
the weight of water unfathomable

but most of the time you are like one of those trick
                                                    taps
suspended over a pond, seemingly unattached
to any supply, but the stream of water
constant, clear, flowing up as well as down,
and me wanting to believe in the magic,
that you can defy gravity, that not all tricks
are in the eye, the sleight of a hand.

CUTTING BACK

A REVIEW OF
THE SORCERER'S ARC
BY JUNE ENGLISH

My favourite poem in June English's collection is
Cutting Back The Delphiniums, two free verse
strophes meditating on a personal relationship
which is suffering from over-zealous pruning. The
verses are strongly rhythmic, and hover on the edge
of classical iambics without quite surrendering to
that regularity. The images are very powerful, and
strongly evoke a situation of domestic tension. The
delphiniums are 'fierce' and

thunderous purple, ragged from the storm;

This line is very nearly an iambic pentameter, and
would be if it had a syllable before 'thunderous.'
As it is, it is vigourously trochaic, with the
emphasis on its first syllable. The play between a
sense of regular rhythm and the breaking of that
rhythm is a powerful reflection of the theme of the
poem, namely how severely to prune the
delphiniums, and how much space the author is
allowed to waste or 'clutter' in her domestic life.
Thus the poem is full of'unruly' lines which refuse
the discipline of iambic pentameter while often
coming close to classical rhythms.

8

>
> the piled-up grievances that chip mugs

flirts with being an iambic pentameter but finally refuses. All it needs is another syllable, say a 'the' before 'mugs' to make it scan. Yet it is left raw, deliberately flattened, scorning the softness of the merely iambic.

The danger of writing free verse which does not engage with classical scansion, in my view, is that it may become indistinguishable from prose, and the poem which faces 'Cutting Back The Delphiniums,' namely 'Make Do And Mend' does run that risk. I'm not able to find the kind of energy, the contained vigour and sense of rhythm which brings 'Cutting Back The Delphiniums' to life. To my mind, for free verse to work, it must be *nearly* classical, but breaking away, interrogating the form. If it moves too far away, how can it be distinguished from prose?

The reader may decide which poems in the collection come close to classical verse, and which stay further away; and some may prefer poems which tend towards the 'free' end of the spectrum of free verse. My own preference is for those poems which retain sense of rhythm, such as 'Limbo,' with its fine opening pentameter:

>
> When sea-mists make life hell for motorists

and its follow-up 'refused iambics:'

>
> and foghorns haunt the becalmed straits

This is free verse at its best.

9

STEVE BAGGS

THREE FRUITS OF LOVE

Tomato

There is too much love in a tomato.
It promises so much,
But it cuts too easily,
Reavealing its ripeness.
Naked in my hand
I squeeze the blood and pips.
It purees like a melting heart.

Orange

An orange is strong.
It will put up a fight
And leave you with sore thumbs.
It will surprise you with its sweetness,
Or make you wince with its acid wit.
The scent will stay with you
Tingling on your fingers
Lingering like a lover's kiss.

Apple

I have never been tempted:
That shiny coat deceives,
Like a brief love affair.
The mystery is in the core
Which frustrates us all
Between finger and thumb.

RONALD BARRETT

THE PASSAGE OF LIFE

Some soar like a rocket
In the blackness of the sky
They explode in a cluster
Brilliant stars
Trailing in its wake
Fast vanishing dots of light
Just as we in our life
reach our zenith and
then fall back to earth
Our brief dazzling display over
Who remembers it now?
The burnt out remains of our rocket
fallen down trodden under the dead leaves
in time to enrich the earth from which it came

*Ronald Barrett lives in Ramsgate, and is a regular at the
EAST KENT POETRY SOCIETY, which meets fortnightly at
the SWALLOW HOTEL in Ramsgate.*

*

*Steve Baggs is reluctant to try to define poetry, but does prefer
more modern, contemporary poetry. His favourite poet is
John Masefield, especially 'Sea Fever.' He lives in Deal.*

GORDON BRENCHLEY

NO RAINBOWS

While on the bus to Tesco's
I saw they'd sunk the Ark.
Not a sight for drinking souls
Each window a metal sheet
Full of little holes.

Like other landmarks in our town –
The Nelson, Steam Packet, Rising Sun,
The Guinea, they've all gone down.

For quantity drinking we lust.
Won't go to the pub on the street.
Cheapest is best – the pennies you save
Plus you're not sure whom
You're likely to meet.

Noah's Ark. Quit the scene have you?
No Ararat or rainbow rising
No olive branch from out of the blue?

I got back home from Tesco's
And four by four
My twelve green cans of lager
Fell clattering to the floor.

Gordon Brenchley is well known on the folk music circuit,
and has set a poem by Sandy Edwards to music, which is
reproduced on the next page.

12

GORDON BRENCHLEY

A SETTING OF SANDY EDWARDS' POEM

AN AGE OLD CHOICE

KAREN BOTTING

FOUR SEASONS

Spring

Blossom-laden boughs
Gentle breezes blowing through
Confetti sprinkles down.

Summer

Tall, golden flowers,
Heads turned towards the sun
Worshipping its warmth.

Autumn

Golden brown leaves fall,
Lazily twirling, floating,
Sculpting crunchy drifts.

Winter

Soft lacy snowflakes,
Tumbling softly, silently,
Turning the world white.

Karen Botting has written sci-fi novels and children's stories, and enjoys writing haiku and other kinds of verse as a diversion. She lives in Herne Bay and is a full-time mum.

HILARY BUSSEY

WHITSTABLE BEACH

… now deserted; sky and sea
reflect steel grey,
the breeze frisky.
I stand beached in
bleak isolation except
for a cormorant
fixed to a post,
held by tenacity.
The wind ruffs his feathers.
We both shrivel visibly.

I stand, and weep loss;
(inwardly)
Press my feet hard to flint
And unforgiving pain of
Oyster shells.
The outer agony obliterates
the inner.
How long I stand?
The tide has turned,
laps my feet,
a soothing cold compress.

*Hilary Bussey lives in Whitstable, and has attended June
English's writing group.*

15

NANCY CHARLEY

RESOLUTION

'Arthur,' she called, 'Oh, God,'
Neither answering I took the liberty,
'Yes darling, what do you want?'
So two deserted bodies intertwined –
hers wrapped in the past, fragments of
another time, mine using her need
to keep me present placed.
Self-pity ebbed by pitying her,
absorbed by loving, caring,
finding new worth in resolving her need.
Until that patient present made
the broken past less raw, less real,
and with her loss, my future came.

*Nancy Charley is a member of the EAST KENT POETRY
SOCIETY, which meets fortnightly at the SWALLOW HOTEL,
Ramsgate.*

JENNI CORBETT

FIRE ON THE BEACH

Primitive ritual of fire on sand
in dark low tide patterns.
The search for meaning
as waves of fire trace
shapes of abstract form.

Not quite a performance
if that is required.
More a happening
an installation prone to
unpredictable occurrence.

Fire on the beach
and the patterns primitive.
Like a Tate Modern art
event in minimal drama
not a bang but a whimper.

It may not be what the crowds
wanted by way of a show.
I liked its spontaneity
In not quite working but being
fascinating in a quiet way.

*Jenni Corbett has a PhD in Sociology, and admires the poetry
of Philip Larkin. She lives in Broadstairs.*

JENNY CROSS

REMEMBERING

Does a fly trapped in amber
remember
the days of golden haze,
the days of mist and rain,
the days of delirious flight?

Trapped in amber, does the fly remember
the days of wine and roses
the days of fermented fruit,
apples, pears, once drunk
made all things possible?

Now, trapped in amber
no forward no back
no upside down
breath less, stuck, fixed
unchanged, unchangeable

Trapped.
The fly remembers.

*Jenny Cross teaches creative writing and runs a reading
group in or near Canterbury. She once ran an antiques
business, and even danced on Top Of The Pops. A rich family
life vies with political activism, and her favourite poem is
'This is just to say' by WC Williams.*

PAUL CURD

MY LONDON

When I think of London I start
at Arding and Hobbs, by the station,
and walk up St John's Hill to the bridge
where they dared me to cross on the wall
through steaming clouds from the trains below.

I press on, past the Saturday morning picture house
where me and my mates were all Grenadiers
and the Monday to Friday of High View School,
and the gap in the houses where the doodle-bug fell,
and All Saints' church where my mum got hitched,
and Wandsworth Common football, skins v shirts.

Then over the river on my favourite bridge,
to Fulham Road Chelsea, and my Saturday Blues.
Up Kings Road, Sloane Square and Pimlico
to Westminster and the indelible shame
of grey flannel shorts
and Whitehall, where I civilly served
and was introduced to opera in English, up the road.

Now through Admiralty Arch to the Mall from
                                          where
I stroll through the parks to Notting Hill
and the number twenty-eight bus
to Westbourne Park,
and your house,
and you.

Paul Curd lives in Ash, near Canterbury.

JULIA CURUMTALLY

GREEN ALCHEMY

In this time of green – wood-pulsing, life sap,
Is the surging in you blocked by bitterness of bile,
Sweet springs of vibrant beauty
Turning inward, acid-burned?

Then, seek stillness, touch the balm of grace.

With hands so softened, reach deep into your wood,
Find the knots of bitterness, hold them tenderly
Until the sickly yellow turns to green –
A bright wild quickening of gratitude.

Julia Curumtally lives in Broadstairs.

*

*Daren Liker is living and working in Canterbury, but returns
regularly to her roots in New England, where she used to
teach creative writing.*

*

*Etelka Marcel used to teach English, but after the death of her
husband took up archaeology, on which she now gives talks.
She lives in Margate, and has had poems published in various
magazines.*

SYLVIA DALY

THE GRANGE

(A makeover – thanks to English Heritage)

A brooding, Gothic crone
crouching on the cliff
in Ramsgate.
Pigeons roosted in her rotting rafters,
crows circled, gulls avoided.

Money came for a facelift.

Shrouded in scaffolding and plastic
the renewal began.

Men swarmed,
hammers rang,
dust rose,
lorries thundered,
time passed.

The cloak of mystery falls,
coyly,
revealing
a towering, stiff neck.
The dusty garment slides further,
teasing us with the sharp cleavage of her eaves,
directing our gaze to
her new, sickly growing body.

Pugin's urban hussy,
flaunting her delights
on the promenade
in Ramsgate.

W.A.G. EDWARDS

A FARM IN NOVA SCOTIA

A backwoods farm in disarray,
with paint all peeled and slats astray,
its roof incontinent,
with creaking floors that bow and sway,
a chimney pot that's bent.

A plague of ants, a blind old bat,
the pussy cat that fled the rat,
roosters running wild,
that canine mut there on the mat
so sleepy and beguiled.

In moonshine days there was a still,
until the Mounties took a swill,
Its tubes lie in the grass,
the bottle dump is that there hill.
Watch out for shards of glass.

Inside the outhouse, pull the chain
to make you think you're in the rain,
admire the wooden seat
while waters gurgle down the drain
right beneath your feet.

Idyllic bliss or icy squat,
where heating ducts soon glow red hot
now rusty, like the stove.
A breezy homestead time forgot,
for some a treasure trove.

JUNE ENGLISH

IN TRANSIT

Prior to death, the body releases endorphins to quell pain and fear...

                            First, the falling forward. Blackout:
flying face downwards through
a cylindrical tunnel, fierce electrical
storms explode around me,
lightning-flashes glance off metal
surfaces, startled fireballs roll, erupt,
the metallic-clang of closing doors
bombards my eardrums,
cyclones blast my cheeks,
whip my hair to rat-tails,
flatten my hands against my thighs
as I torpedo westwards,
portholes thunder shut leaving
me with snapshots, flash card
impressions of past lives, vacant
worlds, a nineteen forties' living-room,
an empty nursery, a cluttered kitchen,
computer stations – scanners, printers – onwards,
gathering speed, past a deserted playground,
a country church, a wooded hillside
thick with snow, towads
                        a chrysanthemum of yellow light.

Twenty, nineteen, eighteen, seventeen,
she's coming back – sixteen, fifteen,
she's almost there, fourteen, thirteen –
my heart pounds, drums against my ribs;
twelve, eleven - the helicopter whirr
of a bee's wings and its body bouncing
off the window, hell bent on escape – *ten, nine,*
come on, you can do it... I open my eyes,
note tubes, drips, the doctors bending over
me; a nurse is rubbing my hands, another
supports me as I turn my face to greet
the sun's warmth, crying
                      for the living hell of it.

POPPY FIELDS

2.30 am

Rain spatters onto the window pane
Glistening from the light of the moon
As it falls from the sky

Wind rushes through the leaves
The clock ticks away
Flowers wither in the vase
Birds slumber

It will soon be dawn
The chorus will start
Breakfast dishes in the sink
Coffee percolating on the stove

*Poppy Fields lives in Margate, and is a regular at Philip
Woodrow's workshops which are held in Corby's Tearooms,
Ramsgate, on alternate Saturdays.*

*

*Sylvia Daly organizes opera recitals in Corby's Tearooms in
Ramsgate – that is when she is not engaged in political
activism!*

*

*June English organizes the **SPLIT THE LARK POETRY
FESTIVAL, which takes place each summer in Dover, Deal
and Sandwich.***

24

CAROLINE FOX

HEMISPHERES

Like Sunday ritual – lifted respectfully
from the shelf – a heavy tea-tray of a book
opens at one familiar page, laid before me
as anatomy – Africa's mons pubis,
South America's flaccid hang. I trace
my finger across continents and oceans –
swirls of fingerprint glide smoothly over
mountains, forests, deserts. You are there,
less than a laser dot of ink, and I am
here, under a cross of longitude and latitude.
It's hard to understand this distance –
how I can span my thumb to little finger
across a line that represents nothing solid –
nothing I could walk into with a bump.
A little like the time you heard yourself described
as 'middle-aged' and wondered when
that silent transition had taken place.

*Caroline Fox lives near Dover, and has brought out a
collection of poems called 'Courting Professor Alzheimer.'
Her website is carolinefox.com*

MAUREEN JONES

MAGNETIC POETRY

I'm sorry I'm in such a state, I've had a busy day.
Some poets just came in and wouldn't go away.
They knew we'd shown an interest in writing poetry
So they all came in for coffee or, if they preferred it, tea.

Auden couldn't make it, he told us when he phoned, [stoned
But Shakespeare brought some lager, and Coleridge was
Sophocles and Plato both enjoyed their herbal tea,
Don't ask what they were on about as it's all Greek to me.

Robert Louis Stevenson turned up in a hat
With a notebook and a donkey, so he stopped to have a chat.
He said 'Do you like Kipling?' Oh how the laughter rippled
As the poets quipped in chorus 'I don't know – I've never
                                      Kippled!'

Chaucer seemed a friendly bloke, although a little crude,
He taught us all some naughty phrases while the coffee
                                    brewed.
We'd sat him next to AA Milne – not such a good idea,
But we'd run out of chairs and had no room for Edward Lear.

Coleridge went on about some really dodgy dreams, [creams.
While Shelley, Keats and Byron handed round the custard
Stevie Smith said not for her as she was on a diet,
And Catullus was in love again, so he was rather quiet.

Betjeman used irony, feet firmly on the ground,
While Walter de la Mare politely passed the sugar round.
Ted Hughes did some powerful stuff, no flowery bits or frills,
But Wordsworth started sulking as we had no daffodils.

Patience Strong just smiled and said how friendship is a
                                    blessing,
But poor old Wilfred Owen couldn't help but be depressing.
Pam Ayres cheered us up though when our spirits took a dive.
She said 'I'm not a classic, but at least I'm still alive.'
                              [continued on p 40]

RACHEL KING

HAIL

The sky is navy
turning black.
Icy balls of hail pour down,
looking like polystyrene,
rock salt,
sherbet pips.
Hitting the guttering
the stones sound like
rustling crisp packets.
They bounce
on the old wooden seat,
speckle the road,
and melt
leaving a maze
of puddles.

*Rachel King defines poetry as 'words which please the mind,'
and likes free verse and haiku saying that free verse 'offers a
great opportunity for expression.' Although she reads poets
like WH Auden, her favourite poem is 'The Highwayman' by
Alfred Noyes. She lives near Whitstable.*

*

*Maureen Jones lives in Lympne, near Hythe, and reads her
poems at the Broadstairs Folk Week.*

JAMES KINGSCOTT

DOOMED YOUTH

As I circle under the folding night,
(While blind kites fly in the bourgeois sky,)
Where once so early we caught passion's flight –
Before we took notice of the aged sigh,
Before we saw our dreams put up for sale go by.
Passion now lies dead on factory floors
Or resting in peace outside office doors.

And cradled this night are yesterday's young
Hearing idle chimes of those singing songs
Whose meaning for them is yet unsung;
But whispering age to the grave belongs, Once they
were young and sang idle songs.
It was once so early they caught passions
So early now abandoned for fashions.

From the pale window light the children hide
To leave spaded hands that curse puppet strings
The children hide in the black bound street side
Victims, embracing material things.
Hiding in history's resounding rings.
For all a suburban anarchist's rant
He'll never sum up time – he can't.

Blind are these steps which send me to retire.
This is Billy Liar,
And the Fall of his Empire.

ODIOUS IDEAS

a Review of

THE ODE LESS TRAVELLED

by

STEPHEN FRY

Some people may not like Stephen Fry's book on poetry, '*The Ode Less Travelled,*' because it proclaims some old fashioned ideas about poetry. But it is a book which is overflowing with knowledge, wit, style and provocative insights. Fry is a natural teacher, and is clearly passionate about his subject.

So what are these old fashioned ideas? The main one is trumpeted in the first chapter, which is on metre. This chapter is headlined with a quote from the American poet JV Cunningham to the effect that *POETRY IS METRICAL WRITING.* To some, this is a red rag to a bull, and indeed such a statement seems to go against the whole trend of modern education, where poetry seems to be defined as 'anything I (write down and) call a poem.' For many people, poetry is about 'authentic feeling' rather than controlled language. Fry's aim

ODIOUS IDEAS

is to remind us that poetry is about the ordering of words to make musical patterns incorporating rhythms and rhymes, and he does this in a wonderfully entertaining way.

Fry explains how the 'natural' rhythms of English contrast with the 'natural' rhythms of other languages, and how early English verse, before Chaucer, reflected natural speech rhythms, while later 'art' verse reflects the influence of classicism, via Latin and French, which puts the emphasis on syllabic counting to make a regular beat. In non-classical English verse, the number of stresses in a line may be constant while the number of syllables may vary. In English classical verse, such as Shakespeare's blank verse, the number of syllables will be constant, as well as the number of stresses. This creates the basis of classical metre, the foot, which is a fixed number of syllables and stresses, as in the iambic foot, which has two syllables and one stress, always on the second syllable. To some this is the meat of poetry, while to others this is horrifying pedantry. From Chaucer to Browning, the dominant 'high art' verse form has been the iambic pentameter, which means a line of five iambic feet, or ten syllables with five stresses. The iambic pentameter has also been a prime target for Modernism, which has sought to replace it with 'Free Verse.' The high priests of non-classical

ODIOUS IDEAS

verse are figures such as Whitman, Hopkins, Pound, Eliot, Lawrence, Williams, Ginsberg, and so on. A major alternative to the iambics of the 'high' English tradition is 'syllabics,' which draws its influences from 'syllabic' languages such as Japanese and French. In this mode, lines are based on syllable counts, not stress-counts. Thus the best known exemplar of the form, the haiku, is a poem of 17 syllables, and any number of stresses, presumably. Fry, with characteristic verve, cannot resist referring to syllabics disrespectfully as 'silly bollocks' because, in his view, a form designed for a syllable-based language has no validity in a language which is stress based, like English, where the reader or listener instinctively seeks out stress patterns, and can only be baffled by the lack of stress patterning in syllabics.

But apart from this controversy, *The Ode Less Travelled* is a treasure house of information about verse forms from Dante's terza rima through Chaucer's Rhyme Royal, the Spenserian stanza, the ballad, the Heroic Couplet, the various forms of ode – Sapphic, Pindaric, Horatian, Lyric, Anacreontic – the Villanelle and the Sestina, to forms so obscure I'd hardly heard of them before. Rhyme and diction are not left out, and neither are the entertaining rants of the author. Altogether very enjoyable.

31

JEREMY LANGRISH

DISTRACTION

Between the seeing and the stare,
between parted lips
is a gasp.

A moment of vacancy
when seeing is not the same
as looking, and looking doesn't matter
(as it were eyes disconnected from head)
what they see is not
what is looked at

Behind the eye hidden –
imaginings
(the eye on the fly
a division of buttock
a resolution of breast)
linger

Looking away
misdirects attention –
to avert the assault in the stare

but it means
I AM TAKING NOTICE
OF YOU

*Jeremy Langrish is a regular at the BROWN JUG poetry
readings in Broadsatirs (every fourth Thursday of the month),
travelling in from Maidstone.*

DAREN LIKER

SUGAR SAGE

I remember her apricot wrinkles
And coolie hat
This china woman
With the river eyes
Who became my sugar sage
In the orange light
With her pole
And two tin pots
Across her pressed
Polished shoulders.
One container held
Almond encrusted cookies
The size of my moon face
The other was a mysterious
Milky lake
That had pink all knowing eyeballs
Floating on its surface.
I would quickly give her
Coins for the biscuit
So that I could move away
From these jelly monsters
That knew my sweet tooth pain.
But then she would give me
A Buddha smile
And the white pebbles
Would crunch
Under our feet
As we parted in the middle
Of the driveway.

ETELKA MARCEL

THE HOSPITAL VISIT

His eyes lit up the morning sky
from grey to blue when he saw me.
His face a transparent white
Let his cheeks' red veins gush away

with the red veins of four tulips'
folded petals stood in green glass.
Hand-blown glass distorting stems
like his hands now combing his hair.

Greying hair, with brown earthworms-
like-fingers which paint history
on hospitals' long corridors.
'Sorry,' he said, 'I've been asleep.'

I said, 'Must have done you good.'
He tried to smile. His mind dipped
with dipped thoughts we often shared
while walking along the shore.

His bed the shore now, crumbs on sheets:
wind-swept sand-dunes as his legs moved.
While his legs moved I saw shells
he trod on looked like mosaics.

Concerned he looked at the racing clouds
with the sky pitching black, threatening
thunder, pitching light and wind's
life-forces against his own.

PHILIP MOSS

PUDDING

The pudding sat on the hedge where I had thrown it.
Cherry bits and custard bits
Chunks of cream

Sister Teresa had informed us
Little black boys in Africa
Would tear each other's arms off
Just to get a spoonful
Of our filthy trifle

We didn't care
We'd rather be in their position
They could change places any day
Come and endure a catholic education
Catechism and filthy trifle

Next Monday morning
Instead of assembly
Followed by double maths
Me and my class
Would stroll across
Africa
Starving
In loin cloths
Instead of school uniform
And we'd be whistling
A happy tune
Because we'd never have
Pudding
Again

JOE PARSONS

IF I WERE

If I were a poet
(Which in my self I cannot be)
I would stand on mountains
And speak my words to the wind

If I were a musician
I would be the man
Standing on the corner
With nothing but a message

If I were a painter
I would paint the sky
That hangs over Canterbury
Using only maroons and silvers

If I were a man
As opposed to boy
I would stand with you
Inside a sunset

Joe Parsons is fifteen and likes Bob Dylan, Artur Rimbaud, Billy Childish and Pete Doherty.

*

James Kingscott is studying at the University Of Kent At Canterbury.

MAGGIE REDDING

TRAGUMNA

(West Cork, Ireland)

Europe's last fingers
stretch out in hunger
only to be battered
and forgotten.

An extremity abandoned,
bereft of warmth, respite
or comfort
is best forgotten.

Storm-thrown stones
lie beached on the peaty shore
of this starving place
of bitter ghosts, forgotten.

Maggie Redding's favourite poem is Yeats's 'Innisfree.'

*

Sandy Edwards has brought out a collection of poems called 'An Antique Place' and lives in Manston, near Ramsgate. He also writes novels and stories.

JASON RUSSELL

IN THE CRYPT OF CANTERBURY CATHEDRAL.

Jovial sincerity – parapet of beauty,
And lingering gazes mocking
In their cruelty.

Surrounded by nothing more than
A congregation of strained gestures.

And the rendered darkness
That slowly festers.

For soulless creatures
Surround this place,
And images disappear so fast
I have no time to contemplate
A place where life and death
Recycle in glee.

Jason Russell, who lives at Chartham, Kent, enjoys soulful poetry, and likes Blake, Keats and Rimbaud, as well as, apparently, Paul Shaw's 'To an Insane Poet.'

*

Lucy Rutter is now doing an MA in creative writing at Oxford.

NO ONE

comments on her
beautiful smile
any more,

she's realised.
She's been spending
a lot of time
soaking
in the bath,
and questioning
her own existence,
contemplating
and examining
her own toes
(ten pink oblongs
at the end of the bath,
decorating,
and occasionally re-
            filling,
the white porcelain,)
dipping her heels,
stretching and
            pointing
at scented drops of
            moisture
through the steamy,
            soapy water.

So when her handsome tom
lands gracefull, suddenly
on all four paws, balanced
precariously,
she blows him a kiss
encouragingly
and he cocks one ear
rakishly
like just one eyebrow raised
flirtatiously.
He sniffs the water,

but even he
sneezes in disgust.
As he pads away firmly,
he turns back
and throws a look
of deep mistrust,
as if to say,
(in tones full of hauteur)
'Really,
do you think you ought to
be *sitting* in that water?'

PAUL SCANLON

THE SOMALI ROAD

I've got blisters on my brain Ma!
The news is boiling over
And she just stands and hand wrings what's
there.
Vacantly she begins to stare
A curled up lip asks are you sure you matter
He mutters let's see if we can reduce it
And begs to suck her tits
The scullery maid slams the kitchen door
And all looks declare with
A tut that they really know
Thigh stroking with shivers in their timbers
They confirm their comfort fears.

*

Maureen Jones's 'Magnetic Poetry' *continued*

So I sip my tepid coffee and I think, it could be worse,
As we sit round all gossiping in sonnet and blank verse,
And rather me than Her-Next-Door, what is a girl to do?
When twenty silent movie stars demand a barbecue.

PAUL SCANLON

SHOE-TIME MAN

Footsteps slapping ground
scrape and step the slab and stone
made fresh for him

The French pickpocket climbs the wooden stairs
smelly carpet undone
the door opens loose
with give in his entry

Walking through his life
his life-walking feet
his tired feet
message pads giving their all

In the sand with water
playfully around
he wriggles his toes.

Paul Scanlon lives in Margate.

*

Philip Moss lives in Seasalter.

41

PAUL SHAW

PERSIAN MINIATURE

The rowan trees have flickering leaves
Like Russian prose which lets light through
The passion of the discourse. Here,
Lemons thrive on southern slopes, with figs
And oranges, that hang like signs
Of God. They glow and carry truths
Like letters from Divinity,
As Ayatollahs carry thoughts
Of Absolutes. The colours of
The foliage show an impulse in
The Universe, a moral voice
Commanding light, yet lions lurk
Behind the rocks, and tigers couch
In grass, in golden grass, as if
The glorious garden, measured by
A subtle eye, must have a flaw,
A wandering Satan testing out
Design. We see the limits of
Divine conception, or of our
Perception in the claws still raised
Above the deer, whose fear is us.
We turn in fright towards the Shah
Whose prowess is recorded in
The margin of the scene, where he
And his retainers bring the power
Of bows to deal with lions' claws.
Their horses rear as bowmen send
A shower of death towards the grass.

SINDONIA TYRELL

SOME THOUGHTS ON MARTYRDOM

(Looking at St George and the Princess by Pisanello)

On the gallows corpses twist and sway.
Castle turrets pierce the blackened sky.
The smiling watchers bow their heads and pray.

The holy ram is sacrificed today.
See the eager crowd all turn their eyes.
On the gallows corpses twist and sway.

Martyrdom is never far away.
A sword that slices truth could show us why
the smiling watchers bow their heads and pray.

Off stage the dragon waits to join the play.
The chosen princess thinks it's time to cry.
On the gallows corpses twist and sway.

Our hero saint knows who he has to slay
but, sheathed, his sword remains beside his thigh.
The smiling watchers bow their heads and pray.

Religion has too high a price to pay
and even saints will turn their backs and sigh
while on the gallows corpses twist and sway
and smiling watchers bow their heads and pray.

43

PHILIP WOODROW

WISH YOU WERE HERE

The postcard lies, arriving one week late.
A rural idyll, taken one fine day.
It rained all week; the blue clouds were all grey.
Still, they pretended that their week was great.
They'd booked ahead, and paid the premium rate
So, having got there, felt obliged to stay.
Their room was adequate. Their holiday
a masquerade they tried to vindicate.

One week away, they followed postcards back
to the big smoke. Back home, they show their
friends
the photos they have taken. No blue skies,
no Shangri-La. They have some cheap nic-nack,
a souvenir, not made there. He pretends
they like it. *Things are fine,* their postcard lies.

Philip Woodrow organizes poetry readings around Thanet,
usually in pubs or cafes where the poetry can be helped along
with a pint or tea and cakes.

*

Sindy Tyrell is a member of the Split The Lark poetry festival
team, and lives in the Deal area.

East Kent Poetry

Society & Journal

Editor
Paul Shaw

SPECIAL FEATURE
FOUR POEMS BY LYNNE REES
Although born in South Wales, **Lynne Rees** has
lived in Kent since 1985, where she ran her own
second-hand bookshop for twelve years. She holds
an MA in writing from the University of
Glamorgan, was awarded a Hawthornden
Fellowship in September 2003, and teaches part-
time on the creative writing programme at the
University of Kent. She's the author of a novel, *The
Oven House* (Bluechrome 2004), and a collection of
poetry, *Learning How To Fall* (Parthian Books
2005), and founder of AppleHouse Poetry – an
independent project supporting poets in Kent and
the South East through a programme of
masterclasses, workshops, and pamphlet and
anthology publication. In 2005/6 she is
representing Canterbury and Kent in Words
Unbound, an international writers' exchange.

EAST KENT POETRY REVIEW

Spring 2006
(Biannual: Spring and Autumn)

Poems and/or critical prose
welcome with SAE to
Paul Shaw
34 Royal Rd
Ramsgate
Kent
CT11 9LE

East Kent Poetry

Society & Journal

For copy of magazine, please send large
envelope with 52p in stamps.

paul@paulshaw24.wanadoo.co.uk
tel 01843 590 235

Price £1.95

EAST KENT
POETRY REVIEW

A Journal of Poetry and Commentary
Serving Thanet, Canterbury, Dover,
and beyond.

CONTENTS

EDITORIAL

In this the first edition of EKPR I hope to reflect the enthusiasm for poetry which exists in our region.

I've invited contributions from people I've met on various occasions during the past few months, especially at sessions of poetry reading held under the auspices of Philip Woodrow at the Brown Jug Inn at Dumpton, and at 'Sandywiches' Café in Northdown Rd, Cliftonville.

I've been asking people for their views on poetry, and indeed handing out 'vox pop' questionnaires, and obtained a wide-ranging set of responses, from those who have a confident belief in the healing power of poetry, to those who see poetry as a craft, a branch of 'Creative Writing,' to those who see their work as 'merely' modest attempts at self-expression.

At what may be called the 'serious' end, there are those who see poetry as a vocation, with rules and purposes, as a search for the beautiful in language, or for social truths, involving all sorts of special things – different kinds of verse forms, a special vision of life, a search for the true self, and so on.

At the less 'serious' end – so to speak –

there are those who enjoy a good rhyme, a humerous anecdote, a risque joke, a roll in the mud, an old-fashioned ballad, an outrageous utterance, a word-feast, and so on.

The vibrancy of the East Kent poetry scene has been noticed recently by the London-based Poetry Review, which has an article describing, amongst others, the work of June English and her indefatigable Deal-centred group, 'Split the Lark,' who have been putting on an excellent poetry festival this summer. June's remit is not only for poetry, but prose as well, as she provides Creative Writing courses, and 'mixed' reading evenings at the Sandwich Bird Observatory on occasional Sunday.

Whitstable has no less than two poetry journals – Barbara Dordi's 'Equinox' and Jane Hardy's 'Connexions.' Broadstairs is home to a performance poetry trio called 'Scatterlings,' who have been giving readings in the bar of the Marlowe Theatre in Canterbury. Ramsgate is host to a group of 'women-oriented' writers (if that is the right term in these post feminist days,) who include Maggie Harris and Felicity Brookesmith, and who meet at Corby's Tearooms on occasional Sunday afternoons.

This edition of EKPR introduces a number of local voices, including our own inhouse Poet In Residence Jonathan Munger, who works in the tradition of EJ Thrib (made famous by his work in Private Eye.)

.

LETTERS TO THE EDITOR

Sir – People who read my poems sometimes complain that I use 'old-fashioned' words, and 'unusual' word order. I say that I like these things and that as I am the writer, I can decide what sort of words I can use. What do you think?

W.E. (Minster.)

Editor – Perhaps it depends on how many people you want to read your work. Readers have rights too!

*

Sir – I remember a poem which was read out at the Brown Jug a few months ago which had the audience rolling in the aisles. It was about a pet haddock, and I'm wondering who wrote it?

F.J.M. (Cliftonville.)

Editor – It was called 'I Had A Haddock,' and was written by Patrick Barrington. The only work of his that I've managed to find on the internet is 'The Diplomatic Platypus.' The chap who read 'I Had A Haddock' at the Brown Jug was the inimitable Charles Wright.

THE   POEMS

SILVER SAPLING

by
Sandra Burdett

A forest silenced by a fall of snow
is absolutely still.
A muted chiaroscuro
of subtle tones until
a glow, surprising
by its very possibility,
from tiny drops on silver sapling
birch, transforms reality.
From every twig a fragile, pendant bead
of moisture, glinting in a single shard
of sun; a crystalline or silver seed.
No rigid icicle, not hard.

This moment can't be pickled, left unmade
In galleries; nature's art will fade.

FROSTY MORNING
by
Paul Curd

I hate the leaving of the morning bed warmth
      for the crisp cold kit
      on the back of the chair.
I hate my running shoes, still caked with mud,
      soggy and damp,
      outside and in.
I hate stepping out the back door to 'warm up,'
      and the breath-taking shock
      of the biting-cold air.
I hate the slip of the ice-hardened mud
      on the well-trodden path
      through the first frozen field.
I hate the treacherous horse-hoof holes
      in the dangerous ground
      with its frost-solid ruts.
Then I'm in my stride, and the sun slips out from its
dull grey quilt
 and black ploughed fields warm to corduroy brown
 and bare-boughed trees become feathers of flame
 and the spire of the church gleams gold on the hill

and I'm chasing my shadow,
      stretched two fields ahead,
and breathing the sun-released smell of the earth,
and I'm racing the dog-walkers' dogs down the hill
      on the well-trodden path
      through the next glistening field.

AN AGE-OLD CHOICE

by
Wm. A. G. Edwards

O that girl who once captured my heart,
My wife she was never to be,
For the woman who drove us apart
Has seduced all resistance from me.

And my darling, with tears in her eyes
On the day that we said our farewell,
Had accepted my tissue of lies
When the truth was too bitter to tell.

And the woman who conquered my soul
In the years when she failed to be true,
Did so readily harvest her toll
As I dreamed of the girl that I knew.

A TOUR OF MASADA

by
Wm A. G. Edwards

I saw Masada on the way
a barren place, dusty,
the fortress of a valiant band
who chose to die.
On the summit where they died,
overlooking the shimmering waters
of the Dead Sea,
I saw the siege lines and the ramp,
and, down below,
a tumbled Roman outpost.
Here, where they took their own lives,
I stood in the sweltering heat
among the tourists, enjoying the day,
while in Jerusalem, another bomb,
another sacrifice.

PIU TORMENTOSO

by
June English

Where are they now, who cried with the willow?
Which way shall I read this myriorama?
Those young English lovers of long ago,

did they build the bowers, creating the tableau
and setting the stage for their great melodrama?
Where are they now, who cried with the willow?

What did they do to deserve this tomorrow,
The damp and decay of this sad panorama,
those young English lovers of long ago?

Under the eyes of the marble gazebo
were there tearful tirades, was there personal
                                        drama?
Where are they now who cried with the willow?

Was she an heiress? Was he a gigolo?
Did he deceive her intending to harm her?
Those young English lovers of long ago –

is this her face in expressionless cameo,
framed in the locket of kismet or karma?
Where are they now, who cried with the willow,
those young English lovers of long ago?

SMALL FRY

by
June English

(The drug Benzedrine was popular in the 1960's)

Yes. I'm childless. A frigid woman, who
WOWS men. A bit of skirt. A known cock-tease,
a tart who shows her boobs and flaunts her knees,
a come-and-get-it, can't-have-it, won't screw;
a man-hater, who honeys up for B's.*
No matter how I scrub and rinse and squeeze,
my dirty knickers won't come clean. It's true.
I'm filth, I'm slime. There's nothing I can do.

Yes. I,m barren by choice. No kid will call
Me mum. I'm damaged goods, a box of tricks,
psychiatrists still try, but I stonewall.
Surf the web, see what some blokes do for kicks
castrate them slowly ball-by-bloody-ball.
My father broke me in when I was six.

*N.B. Beatrix Campbell – journalist: on Child Abuse:
'Children's bodies aren't like automobiles with the assailant's
fingerprints lingering on the whell. It is the perfect crime.'

GIVE A DOG A HOME

by
Poppy Fields

I'll eat only as much as I need
Some water would help out too
But I'd need to go for a walk
Especially when I need the loo

I'll wag my tail when you come home
I'll lie by your side in the night
I'll even make sure you feel safe
Just in case you might have a fright

I'll lick your tears away when you cry
And comfort through thick and thin
My loyalty to you I'll reward
Our kinship will be a win-win

So your home will be my home to me
When you're out I'll make sure I stay
Inside where it's cosy and warm
And on my warm bed I shall lay

So when you pass by me and see
That I have no home where I can go
That you come in and ask the kind lady
I'm sure that she'll say I can go

FIRST LOVE

by
Marion Nelson

Portobello Road
face in the crowd
thunderbolt hits my heart
is it him?
Crowd hold me
dark moments, panic.

Memories flood back
another place and time
summer warmth – music nights
softness of your lips
love in your eyes
blissfull surrender.

He's out of sight
have I lost him?
Please, not a second time
I fight through the crowd
I'm within reach
wanting the dream.

Trembling I hesitate
with breathless courage
I touch him
call his name
he turns, his blue eyes hold me
eyes of a stranger.

OLD (COFFEE) GROUNDS

by
Lucy Rutter

From the pot she's
neglected to wash,
the sudden forgotten
smoky
smell, the
naughty-
late-night-
cups-of-coffee
smell, the
too-much-
drinking-
endless-talking-
all-about-nothing-
forgotten smell, the
ashtrays-brimming-
wine-stained-glasses-
marmite-toast-crumbs-
sudden, forgotten smell, the
Oh-god-it's-getting-light-out-
side-is-that-the-birds-I-can hear-
smell, suddenly remembered in an
astonishing moment.

LULL

by
Lucy Rutter

The strimmer screams a war cry then chugs
around the armour-plated artichokes,
mashing stalks, dispersing seeds,
insidious little bombs in manure.

The sun encroaches. Grass is cancelled, flattened.
M y arms, vibrating, lengthen.
Clouds fan out,
field mushrooms in a bowl.

The girl is young, unlocks the gate,
saunters down to chop at chunks of earth,
sun-baked; bashes
with her fork with its bent prongs.

I lie on clods, the thistles at my back
and watch her bend and straighten
slim and tall against the sky.
She's planting a volcano in the soil.

That still and earthy, grassy smell must be her skin!
Her form fills up the blank, white sky for me,
hair like black handwriting,
a joined-up n in and.

A KILLING IN RAMSGATE

by
Paul Shaw

The birds are wheeling over Ramsgate's roofs.
Maroons have boomed.
The gulls patrol their base
Then crash land on a chimney ledge.
The threatening sound enlarged
Their scope for minutes in the sky.

A face behind a wire muses, mute
On something like a TV murder, startled by
A kind of boom, an act
Of thunderous horror, leaving
Clues which make a story.
High above, no birds are wheeling,
Only there is oceanic music, as
Of turning spheres.

Is this a trail of blood all down the steps
Beside the harbour, causing gulls
To circle, or the sign
Of sounds resounding in the sky?

TO AN INSANE POET

by
Paul Shaw

Rambling and obscure and beautiful,
Your sonnets lack rhyme yet breathe
With living song. You choose the famous dead,
Portray their veins, their dining jackets, how
They drawled or yelled. And so well-read
You can't resist the gorgeous quote
And veiled references. But deepest gift
Is your involvement with the animal,
The pulse, the lizard eye,
The fervent coitus, and all stages
Of the losses and the rages
Under your sublime calm. Those flow-
On lines, those feeling- flows, your life
Unboundaried, are whisperings of love.

CLIFF FALL

by
Sindonia Tyrell

The devil finds work for an idle mind
on a cliff-top walk in the stuttering sun.
A shimmer on the sea like a shattered mirror.
I lay among the yellow samphire and kidney vetch
you stood close to the edge framing that perfect
                                        shot.
The camera shutter whirred like a bug in my ear.
Clouds performed a partial eclipse.

I heard the gritty rumble of a landslip,
                kept my eyes shut
and imagined you cart-wheeling arse over tip
in a shower of chalk, part of the debris, a man-slide.
Gulls swooped and shrieked, damp grass licked
                                    my cheek.
Oh shit! I've dropped the camera.

DON'T TRY AND TELL ME WHAT TO DO

by
Sindonia Tyrell

When offered odd advice, tossed like pebbles
into the pool of my problems, my muscles tense
like the tawny flank of a vixen scenting prey,
I skeeter from acceptance to discord
and uneasiness lies about my throat
like a silken rope that gently tightens.
So what if galaxies gutter like candles
we'll still all be stars on car-crash TV.

OPTICAL ILLUSION

by
Lyn White

I take the vase
feel its weight
how the neck opens to a 'v'
juts back just before the chrystal
blooms to full-bellied
circumference and, as if the blower
slowed and eased the breath
I followed a gentle taper
to the base.
I wash it like a heavy baby
careful not to graze it on a tap
careful soap can't slither it
from my grasp, pass it
with a tender roll
beneath a cool stream
rinse inside and out, drain
polish to transparency
fill the vessel watch
water fall, settle
catch light and split it
rest confined, nestled
in bright illusion
shaped by boundaries
almost invisible;
glass containing
what cannot be contained,
hesitate to ruin art
by adding flowers.

DARK CARNIVAL

by
John Williams

I leave the dust and smoke of ages past
and with a pitted eye seek innocent horizons.
The dead dry blood has taken on a parchment hue
and is now part of some great passing on.

O for light beyond dusk, to point a better path.
The empty chalice, the false altar
Of past faiths, the sombre songs
To gods of yesterday - what good are they?

Bright carnivals become the mute black funeral.
The weight of the grave does not recall
The paths our footprints trod, now weeded up.
Our garlands lie in dust.

Our trials have one end only –
An empty shell discarded by – who knows?

DESERT CARAVAN

by
Sylvia Daly

Moving slowly but with purpose,
drawn across the burning sand,
direction taken as by magnet,
instinct leads to better land.

Some seem born to travel, landless,
stretch their souls and seek no rest,
have constant learning of the other,
life a never-ending test.

Others, rooted, grow and prosper,
sucking life-blood from the soil,
harvesting their gains and assets,
amassing prizes for their toil.

Fleeting is the nomad's visit,
touching light the earth's rich crust,
experience the unseen treasure,
life's lesson – in the self to trust.

PAN – PIPES

by
Sylvia Daly

It's every town on a rainy day,
people under leaden skies.
Raindrops in the puddles play,
muffled are tha vendor's cries

The group of foreign rainbow men
perform a song from mountain air.
The notes from pipes, like wisps of smoke
escaping in the drizzled blur.

The rhythm pulsing, every step
an insult to the greying light.
The song a culture unrefined,
of wild, intoxicating flight.

I saw them in the town today,
those rainbow men with pipes and rhyme.
I felt them in my heart's strong beat,
the gloom dispelled a fleeting time.

VOX POP PROFILE

by Sylvia Daly

What sort of poetry do you like?   Poetry that deals with life's problems, life's dilemmas and vaguaries.

What is your definition of poetry?   To quote Wordsworth – 'Emotion recollected in tranquillity' – I cannot better this.

Who was the last poet you read ?   Lorna Goodison – her poem 'This is a Hymn.'

Do you have a favourite poet or poem? – Who/What?   Yes, Carol Ann Duffy – I think her work is 'real.'

What do you think about free verse? – Please explain.   I would love to write free verse – I feel trapped by rhyme.

Do you mind your views being printed in the EKPR?   Not at all, that would be great!

TWO POEMS BY PHILIP WOODROW

FINDING A WAY

The map predates Beeching.
It was my parents'. They
younger then than I am now.
It guided them through holidays,
year after year, always the same.
They grew familiar with its fading contours,
Their skins yellowing like the paper.
Their holidays years are over
and the train line traced in red
no longer exists. I trace a casual finger
through towns I barely remember.
We stayed where the paper folds,
now worn to a hole.
The barely perceptible legend
betrays a cocoon of time.

SID TAKES SENNA

& covers my car
with seagull crap.

I wash it clean –
a gleaming target.

Sid flies again

THE FRILL-NECKED LIZARD

by
Charles Wright

The harmless, naked lizard waits alone
Exposed beneath the sun to make him quick.
He sees a shadow flicker on his stone,
Presaging death. In time's proverbial nick
Hawk hesitates a second in the air
As lizard flares his frill, his mouth agape,
His forelimbs raised, his eyes a thwarting glare,
On Charlie Chaplin legs makes his escape.
       This excellent reptile demonstrates to man
       The parable of a survival plan.

When, in the desert of my squandered years,
The shadow flickers on my chosen rock,
I'll throw my collar up about my ears
To greet the bomber pilot with a shock.
I'll ape a black hole with my toothless jaw,
I'll flail defiance at the plunging doom
And crouch with you beneath the desert floor.
Together we shall hear the seismic boom.
       'Nothing to give concern,' I'll say,
                 taking your hand,
      'Just Nemesis nose-diving in the sand.'

COMMENTARY

REVIEW

POETRY ON THE RADIO
by
Paul Shaw

'Poetry on the radio' really means 'POETRY
PLEASE' on Radio 4 on Sunday afternoons at 4..30
– or at least it did until the arrival of the
'ONEWORD' channel on digital radio, which has
wonderful POETRY FILLERS between its main
programmes, which are mostly readings of novels,
thrillers, biographies, or autobiographies.

Occasionally ONEWORD has a main
programme featuring a play by Shakespeare, broken
up into 15 minute slices. Recently, I heard the
entire sonnets of Shakespeare read over several
days in 15 minute slots, and it was an absolute eye-
opener – or rather an ear-opener! I've never been a
big fan of the sonnets, because I've always read
them silently, with the eyes only – but their magic is
in the sound – as I discovered by listening without
looking at the words on the page. The actor-reader
wove a wonderful web of sound and meaning – and
I especially liked Sonnet 98 –'From you have I been
absent in the spring,' a poem which hitherto had
meant little to me. Shakespeare comes alive in the
sound of the words, and the often obscure and
tortuous reasonings of the sonnets become
secondary to the lovely music of the language.

The trouble with POETRY FILLERS is that you can only hear them by accident, but 'POETRY PLEASE' can be accessed easily, and I've just been enjoying Roger McGough's presentation of the theme of parodies. Last week it was poems by 'Anon,' and before that the theme was 'water,' which introduced me to a wonderful poem by Larkin about how he would invent a new religion by using water.

The rareness of poetry in the media cannot be glossed over, and its almost complete absence from TV is a shame. Admittedly, poetry is an aural rather than a visual art, yet poetry in performance – from Shakespeare to Zephaniah can be riveting all-round entertainment.

But at least we have Radio 4 and ONEWORD – and I only wish there was some way of finding out when poetry fillers are going to be used. Perhaps some compilation could be made and broadcast as a programme?

VOX POP

When I handed out questionnaires to people at poetry sessions, I was interested to see what sort of poetry people were reading at home, and what they thought poetry was.

The names that came up in answer to the question, Who is your favourite poet? surprised me because I wasn't familiar with many of them, such as Joshua Clover, Jorie Graham (are they American? Yes, I've discovered,) Nick Laird, Rose Auslander, Harry Clifton.

Names I am familiar with included June English, Mimi Khalvati, Michael Laskey, Lynne Rees, Sylvia Plath, Roger McGough, Wordsworth, Rupert Brooke, Wilfred Gibson.

People's definitions of poetry tended to be succinct, as in 'joy,' 'feeling,' 'a moment,' 'an essence of experience,' 'word-smithing,' or 'a mood.' But some offered a more extended definition, such as 'a small (or large) machine made out of words (which moves one,)' - or – 'a fine art in which the written word is arranged to pass a meaningful message or emotion with a harmony similar to music and in keeping with traditional rules including essentially rhythm, meter and sometimes rhyme.

CONVERSATION PIECE

A poem by our Poet In Residence, Jonathan Munger (aged 51 and a bit,) on the sad death of the actress Anne Bancroft.

LINES ON THE DEATH OF ANNE BANCROFT

So. Farewell Lady Anne,
The Mrs Robinson of film and song,
The poster-lady temptress
Who didn't need to wear a thong
Or blink your eyes behind a fan
To make us graduates
Wish you were our mistress.
You made us pilots
Of uncounted moon-shots,
Space-probes into outer space
In search of someone with your face
And lovely stockinged legs
Arched over mirrors of ourselves.
Farewell seductress,
Farewell Lady Anne,
Who made a boy a man.

TWO WAYS OF READING POETRY

A Review
by
Alan Milne

POETRY: THE BASICS
by Jeffrey Wainwright,
pub. Routledge, 2004.

52 WAYS OF LOOKING AT A POEM
by Ruth Padel
pub. Vintage, 2004.

These two books on poetry are very popular
and very good. Although written by the
distinguished Professor of English at
Manchester Metropolitan University, 'The
Basics' has a lightness of touch and a charm
which makes it a delight to read. '52 Ways'
is perhaps a heavier undertaking, and may
be spread out over a year to reflect its origin
in a weekly newspaper article examining a
different poem each week. Be that as it
may, Ruth Padel offers a very close reading
of 52 poems by a galaxy of contemporary
poets, concentrating on different aspects of
prosody with each poem. Thus Jo
Shapcott's sonnet 'Mrs Noah' gives rise to
an extended description of the formal

qualities of sonnets throughout history, with a technical description of different kinds of rhythm, as well as a thorough analysis of the 'word music' of the poem itself.

Professor Wainwright, on the other hand, begins with a general concept, such as 'Tones of Voice' or 'Rhyme and Other Noises,' and adduces a wonderful range of examples to consider all aspects of the concept. From the unusual beginning where poetry is related to space (yes, space,) through illuminating insights into the origins and justifications of free verse, to the final examination of airy concepts like inspiration and imagination, Professor Wainwright proves to be an enchanting guide to so many delicate aspects of poetry.

In focusing on the work of specific poets, Ruth Padel identifies major trends in modern poetry in English, cuch as the 'decentering' of England as the origin of much English verse. Although there has never been so much poetry published in England as there is now, very many of those poetr hail from elsewhere, such as Derek Walcott from the Caribbean, Fleur Adcock from New Zealand, Les Murray from Australia, and, of course, many distinguished voices from the two Irelands, Scotland, the USA, and even new voices from Eastern Europe. This contrasts with the 'classical' repertoire which Professor Wainwright draws on to illustrate his themes. Thus translations of poets from ancient Greece and Rome, as well as Medieval Europe, rub shoulders with English and American stalwarts to provide a mapping of poetry in the West. But this is not to say that non-western models are excluded, as less well-known forms such as the Arabic ghazal are also described. The adaptation of this two-line form, with its melancholy subject-matter and 'limited range of topic and imagery' (p127) by the English poet Judith Wright is referred to in a discussion which also includes the work of the better-known Japanese poet Basho, author of 'The Narrow Road To The Deep North,' who also provides a model for Judith Wright, whom Professor Wainwright quotes at some length, to illustrate the growing influence of non-western literatures.

Perhaps the most noticeable difference between these two guides to poetry, apart from the formal structures of the two books, is the clear political emphasis given by Ruth Padel, as opposed to the more aesthetic approach of Professor Wainwright. Thus Ruth Padel is eager to describe poetry in terms of political developments, and adopts an undeniably left-wing point of view as she celebrates the growth of regionalism and the developments of feminism, noting that 'it is often said that bad politics make good art.' The work of Carol Ann Dufy is held up as an influential example of 'dramatic monologues which tackled the abuse of power' (p21.) Noting that this form was not new, and citing Robert Browning, CP Cavafy, UA Fanthorpe and Philip Larkin as forbears, Padel praises Duffy's work as 'witty, hard-hitting voicings' which provide 'a poetic comment on her time' (p21.)

The glittering surfaces of consumerist Britain are identified by Padel as influencing the virtuoso imagery of Simon Armitage,'whose first collection was called Zoom!' (p23.) The emptiness and cynicism of advertising, as well as 'Thatcherite injustices' are reflected in the poetics of juxtaposition, where, for example, the televised images of violence may be interspersed with images of ordinary daily life. This technique is rooted in the work of modernists such as Ezra Pound and TS Eliot. But Padel also identifies a major new source of influence for British poetry: Eastern Europe, naming poets such as Herbert, Popa,

Milosz, Holub, Akhmatova, Mandelstam, and Tsvetaeva. Elaine Feinstein is described as the producer of 'trailblazing translation' (p25.) The trend towards self-publishing in Britain is associated with the practise of 'samizdat' in countries where oppressive regimes prevent the publication of authentic poetry. 'Samizdat,' or underground publishing, has been used by many poets to get their voices heard, and many poets in Britain today are seeking to circumvent the 'London-Oxbridge circuit,' and are turning towards new publishing centres in Newcastle (Bloodaxe), Manchester (Carcanet), and Wales (Seren).

Readers of a 'traditional' disposition may not agree with all of Ruth Padel's aesthetics / politics, but her prose is clear and stimulating, her ideas perceptive and wide-ranging, and her passion for poetry is undeniable. Some may prefer the more detached and contemplative tone of Professor Wainwright, who provides a fascinating tour of the world of poetry. Taken together, these two fine books provide endless information, insight and stimulation, and should grace the shelves of anyone who enjoys and cares about poetry.

THE
CONTRIBUTORS

ETELKA MARCEL

Born and educated on the continent, Etelka began
writing at the age of six. She completed her studies
at Hammersmith School Of Art, where she became
reunited with her father after being separated by the
Nazi reign of terror. She then went on to qualify as
a draughtswoman.

Etelka has written one novel, which
unfortunately did not survive the Russian
occupatiuon, and is still working on an
autobiography. Following the death of her husband
and the departure of her daughter from home,
Etelka has been able to devote more time to writing,
although this has to compete with other activities
such as being an EFL teacher and taking a Diploma
in archaeology at Canterbury University. She now
gives illustrated talks on archaeology, as well as
contributing powerful socially engaged poems at the
'SandyWiches' poetry readings.

LYN WHITE

Lyn lives in Maidstone and works part-time as
librarian for the Guest Library at the Carmelite
Friary in Aylesford. Her work has been published
in 'Equinox,' 'Poetry Nottingham,' 'Orbis' and the
anthology 'The Ticking Crocodile' published by
'Blinking Eye,' 2004.

JUNE ENGLISH

June is the indefatigable creator and organizer of the
Split The Lark Poetry Festival, which ran fromJune
to October of this year, and which gave us the
opportunity to meet editors, published poets, and
fellow scribblers. 'Split The Lark,' by the way,
refers to a poem by Emily Dickinson which
suggests that analysing poetry is like splitting a lark,
and June is also involved not only in analysing
poetry, but also prose in her creative writing classes.
Her latest book is called 'The Sorcerer's Arc,' and
may be purchased from this publication for £7..95
plus 40p postage. June has been widely published
in many poetry journals, and her periodical readings
at the Sandwich Bird Observatory involve both
published writers and local voices.

SINDONIA TYRELL

Sindy is involved in running Split The Lark events
with June English and is a regular reader at the
Sandwich Bird Observatory soirees. Of her poetry,
she remarks that 'A lot of my stuff seems to have a
bit of a bite to it lately.'

LUCY RUTTER

Lucy is a lecturer in English who has 'an absolute passion' for reading and writing poetry – to say nothing of short stories and novels. So much so that she has decided to work part time in order to devote more time to writing. Her taste in poetry could be described as inclusive, as it runs 'really from Chaucer to Shakespeare right through to very modern, experimental poetry.' As for a definition of poetry, Lucy quotes William Carlos Williams' idea that 'A poem is a small (or large) machine made out of words,' but adds that 'it also has to move one.' Currently, Lucy's favourite poem is 'The Courtyard' by George Szirtes.

JOHN T. WILLIAMS

John's main interest is in prose, particularly historical prose, as he is the Chair of the Margate Historical Society, as well as archivist of the Manston Aviation Museum. But as a wide-ranging reader of literature, John occasionally turns his hand to the poetic side.

PHILIP WOODROW

Philip lives in Broadstairs, and teaches Nursing Studies. A keen organizer and fan of modern realist verse, Philip runs a whole range of poetry events in Thanet, including poetry workshops, performance poetry in pubs, and what you might call 'chamber' poetry readings and discussions in cafes. Philip likes free verse, and animated, engaged conversations, as well as motivating others to give poetry a try. Now that the Broadstairs Cultural Centre seems to have gone offstream, Philip gives poetry appreciation sessions in his own home, but new venues are always welcome!

CHARLES WRIGHT

Charles is a popular reciter and singer at poetry readings in Thanet. His views on poetry are almost shamanic, seeing it as a healing art capable of uplifting the mind. His performance work is certainly entertaining and much admired, and he is known to many as 'The Chameleon Poet,' as a result of a memorable reading of his poem 'The Chamele

JONATHAN MUNGER

Jonathan is a distinguished poet of the people, writing poems to order in any situation, like a user-friendly poet laureate. He has declaimed on many local radio stations, most recently on Mid-Glamorgan NHS Network, using a kind of Anglo-Welsh to illuminate the lives of immigrants and asylum-seekers. Jonathan loves rhyme and political correctness, and is currently chilling out in Ramsgate.

SANDY EDWARDS

Sandy is a retired engineer living in Manston and is currently working on a novel, as well as a collection of short stories. On top of that, he is also bringing out a slim volume of poems, called 'An Antique Place,' (published by Trafford.com) which may be obtained from this journal, price £6.95, plus 40p postage. Sandy prefers traditional verse forms, saying he 'doesn't quite know what to make' of free verse, as his own poems are lovingly crafted over many years, in an endless search for a rhyme or a word order which perfectly fits the form. As he says, 'I'm an engineer who loves to build poems.'

PAUL CURD

Paul is studying English at Nottingham University, but still rooted in East Kent – just outside Canterbury, in fact. He says he likes all kinds of poetry, but especially likes rhythm. The last poet he read was Roger McGough, and his favourite poem is (probably) Wordsworth's 'Westminster Bridge.' He likes attending poetry events, such as June English's 'Meet The Editors' Day at Deal Town Hall.

PAUL SHAW

Editor of this mag, Paul says that the EKPR is stretching his computer skills to the limit. Having formerly taught English as a foreign language abroad, Paul is now living in Ramsgate and doing freelance work. He enjoys writing poems, attending poetry readings, and talking to people about poetry.

EAST KENT POETRY REVIEW

Autumn 2005

Poems and/or critical prose
welcome with SAE to
Paul Shaw
34 Royal Rd
Ramsgate
Kent
CT11 9LE

email paul.shaw38@btinternet.com

Price £1.95